the LAST YEARS OF CLASS 25s

BARRY J. NICOLLE

LONDON
IAN ALLAN LTD

Cover: On Tuesday 1 May 1984 one of the last 15 boiler-fitted Class 25 locomotives, No 25.044 (now allocated to Carlisle Kingmoor TMD), was seen approaching Old Oak Common West Junction off the joint line. It was on a saloon special organised for Mr W. McAlpine, and it ran as 1Z26, an 11.18 St Pancras-St Pancras service, and travelled over various cross-London lines. *Clive Barlow*

Previous page:
A rake of four loaded airbraked Sealion ballast hoppers emerge from New Mills tunnel on 9 July 1978, behind 25.327. This locomotive, the last in the series, is now, sadly, withdrawn. *N. Johnston*

All uncredited photographs were taken by the author.

First published 1985

ISBN 0 7110 1492 2

Published by Ian Allan Ltd, Shepperton, Surrey; and printed by Ian Allan Printing Ltd at their works at Coombelands in Runnymede, England

Preface

Had the Midland Railway still existed in the 1960s, it would have approved of the BR Sulzer Type 2 locomotives. Small, punchy and with an ability to handle a wide variety of duties, they seemed to be the natural successors to the long line of Midland and LMS medium-powered locomotives. In the early and mid-1960s, the appearance of a gleaming green Sulzer Type 2 spelt an end to many a steam locomotive, and the 327 members of what eventually became BR Class 25 easily replaced twice their number of steam locomotives.

The Class 25 locomotive evolved from Derby's first essay into Type 2 design, the 151 members of Class 24. With the original 'pilot scheme' aims of gentle diesel introduction abandoned, the headlong rush into full dieselisation preceded service evaluation, and this is reflected in the Class 25. The harsh wind of experience blew in the faces of the designers and some of the mistakes made in the Class 24 design were rectified for the '25s', but it didn't stop at D5151 (25.001). There were several basic variations in the 'standard' '25' design, and there were several builders of the class which appeared from Derby, Darlington and the famous Gorton works of Beyer Peacock, between 1961 and 1967.

In the late 1960s another 'harsh wind', one of cost evaluation, began to blow and it was directed at the whole BR diesel fleet. The National Traction Plan saw an end to many small or uneconomic classes by 1971, and Class 25 had the chance to spread its wings. With the demise of the Class 17 Clayton and the Class 29 North British locomotives, '25s' were more prominent in Scotland, whilst down in South Wales and the West Country they replaced diesel-hydraulic locomotives and completely ousted the Class 22 North British version. In native London Midland territory the class was as strong as ever and only on the Eastern Region did its tenuous hold wane, as the indigenous Class 31 took a regionwide grip. The Southern Region never felt the need for the '25s', being plentifully supplied with its very own Class 33 Sulzer Type 3 locomotives.

Throughout the 1970s the '25s' seemed to roam all over Britain, but the responsibility and costs of maintaining the BR Sulzer classes was causing concern, and as the Type 2 classes thinned out, thoughts were turning to the Sulzer classes for future withdrawal. This began in 1975 with the earlier Class 24. With many esoteric design features common to both BR Sulzer Type 2 classes, the pay-back from repairing some Class 25 locomotives was not worth the effort and cost needed. But, it was the industrial recession of 1979/80 that provided the real spur to start withdrawing the '25s' in earnest, and since then the pace of withdrawal has been merciless, only abating when the rate of scrapping exceeded the supply of suitable replacements. Like every class of locomotive the '25s' had an Achilles's heel and this was undoubtedly the traction motor. However, it should be remembered that the class has survived for over two decades, which puts the matter in perspective.

With the decision taken to withdraw the Class 25, by the end of 1977, 309 still remained. The following totals illustrate the rate of withdrawals at the year ends: 1981-205; 1982-164; 1983-119. An upsurge of traffic in 1984 actually witnessed several '25s' reinstated into service which explains why by the end of 1984, 100 still remained. One of the saddest sights on a railway is that of a class in decline. As the once proud and numerous class is reduced in numbers the survivors became more and more unkempt. The paintwork fades and peels, old numbers show through and niggling faults abound. The lines of unserviceable and withdrawn examples collect at depots, forlornly awaiting the final call to the scrapyard.

Such is the fate at present befalling the Class 25. No more can its distinctive roar be heard the length and breadth of the country, and at the time of writing, replacement on its last region (the London Midland) is well advanced. In the not too distant future we shall witness the final specials, the final squeezing of their last drop of usefulness, and we shall be left with just memories.

Memories of what? To many drivers a draughty and leaky locomotive that nevertheless had good acceleration and lightness of control. To many fitters, a locomotive that was not easy to work in and a contortionist's nightmare when it came to taking equipment in and out. And to the ordinary 'gricer', a familiar, almost too familiar locomotive that seemed to pop up everywhere on just about everything.

If we have not mentioned their recent workings that is because this book tells this phase of their history. If you are reading this long after the class is gone, and missed the class completely, try to imagine the throaty Sulzer sound through the next, all too few pages. If, like us, you do remember the sight and sound of these honest locomotives, we hope this book will trigger off a few of your special memories of this unsung, but not forgotten, class.

Andrew Wylie
Murray Brown

Acknowledgements

My personal thanks are extended to my colleagues, Howard Johnston, Murray Brown and Andrew Wylie, without whose extensive help and encouragement this volume would never have got off the ground. Many thanks too, to Peter Kynaston, whose many photographs have, I hope, helped make this book especially pleasing to the eye. In addition, Russel Carter requires a special mention for providing me with a set of his fine line drawings.

Finally, I should like to thank my wife, Liz, and my children, Ben and Stephanie, for putting up with my somewhat eccentric ways over the years.

B. J. Nicolle

Introduction

The British Railways standard Class 25 as we know it today is a direct descendant of the original 1955 pilot scheme order for 20 Bo-Bo diesel-electric Type 2 locomotives. The design originated at Derby, although subsequent batches were built in the railway works at both Crewe and Darlington and also privately at Gorton near Manchester in the Beyer Peacock works. When the production line was eventually completed during 1967, a massive 478 locomotives had been built of either 1,160 or 1,250bhp. Such a figure has only been surpassed by the Classes 08 and 47. When the TOPS computerised numbering system was introduced during the early 1970s, the Type 2 Bo-Bo fell into two main groups; Class 24s, originally numbered D5000 to D5150 and Class 25s, originally D5151 to D5299 and D7500 to D7677. This volume deals with the latter class, the '25s', which entered service between April 1961 and May 1967.

Design

When BR first began to look for equipment for its medium power Derby and Crewe built Type 2 Bo-Bos, the successful Sulzer 6LDA power unit of 1,160bhp with Type 137BY traction motors, was an obvious choice, and Class 24s were thus equipped. The first series of Class 25s were uprated to 1,250bhp, but with similar 137BX traction motors, and it was not until D5176 that the final form of traction equipment, the now famous AE1 253AY motor, was installed. The increase in power was achieved by the introduction of intercooling. The more powerful engine meant a raising of speed from a top speed of 75mph with the Class 24s, to 90mph; and the use of new materials for bearings extended the gap between overhauls to unprecendented levels.

The first 233 Type 2 locomotives (ie all Class 24 and some 82 Class 25s) were built with a pair of doors on the cab fronts to enable the firemen/driver's assistant to reach and operate the boilers of a second locomotive when they were working in multiple. These doors are no longer operational on the remaining members of the class because they caused the cab to be so draughty that they were ordered to be welded up during works overhauls. The only exception is No 25.051 which still has doors at one end. All but the first 20 of the class were built with bogies incorporating SKF roller bearing axleboxes, which proved to be very successful.

Although only 12 members of the class (Numbers D7658-D7669) were built with train air brakes, a large proportion was eventually converted during works classified repairs to incorporate this facility, to cope with the increasing number of company block, Speedlink, and other air-braked services, which were being introduced to the BR network.

None of the class was ever considered for electric train heat conversion (as locomotives), and those not fitted with the standard steam vapour steam generator have a concrete ballast weight to compensate. The main fuel tank is external and hangs between the bogies around the battery boxes, which slide on rollers to give easier access. Water tanks on boiler fitted members of the class are found both underslung next to the fuel tanks, and internally near the heating cubical.

External changes in appearance due to the discontinuation of fitting cab gangway doors, the fitting of various types of roof-mounted, four-character indicator bodies, and the change to the type of body side design incorporating roof vents instead of side ones: all add even more variations to the theme. For guidance, the Class 25 falls into the following batch variations: Nos 25.001-25.082 (D5151-5232) and 25.218-25.247 (D7568-7597) have the original bodyside grille style, front gangway doors (most of which have been welded up) and roof-mounted indicator boxes (although 25.001-25.025 never received the accompanying warning horns beside their boxes). Nos 25.083-25.217 (5233-7567) and 25.248-25.327 (7598-7677) have the newer style body sides with a maximum of two grilles, they were not fitted with the gangway doors, but did have the regulation four-character indicator boxes and associated warning horns.

Certain hybrids have appeared from time to time as a result of collision damage repair, and the Derby works' practice of swapping cabs during works classified repairs.

All Sulzer-engined locomotives fitted for

multiple working come into the blue star coupling category, and can be worked in multiple with up to three fellow members of the class. It was, however, found that when members of the Class 25/3 subdivision were put in multiple with any other Class 25 variation, the trailing load had to be reduced accordingly so as not to exert unneccessary strain on the traction motors.

Allocation

The first batch of Class 25s went with the last four Class 24s to the North Eastern Region, and joined fellow locomotives at Gateshead, Thornaby and Leeds Holbeck depots. By early 1963 No D5176 was allocated to York, and these together with those from Thornaby were regularly seen working other depots' steam locomotive turns. In the summer of 1966 the '9F' steam locomotives on the Tyne Dock to Consett iron ore trains, were replaced by pairs of Type 2 Bo-Bos from Gateshead depot. By 1965 Tinsley had received an allocation of 25 Class 25s, Nos D7624-D7649 which worked from various local depots and had been built by Beyer Peacock Gorton Ltd. In 1964 the firm had won an order for the last 54 locomotives from D7624 to D7677, with which they hoped to keep the locomotive side of their works open. However, they later had to ask to be relieved of the building of the last 18 engines. The workmanship on the privately built locomotives was second to none, and those particular members were rightly called the best of the class.

During its lifetime the class has been allocated to every Region except the Southern. However, at the end of 1964 seven Class 25 locomotives were loaned to Hither Green to supplement the arrival of their own Class 33s. These engines (D5240-45 and D5247), stayed for only three months, and during that time mostly deputised for Class 71 electric locomotive failures. D5186-89 were the first batch of new '25s' to arrive on the London Midland Region and did not do so until March 1963. These were followed in much larger numbers in subsequent years. Although the Scottish Region received a large allocation of second series Class 24s from new, it was not until April 1966 that they received their first Class 25s from the series three batch, Nos D7611 to D7613. These were quickly followed by D7614-D7623, and were all fitted with cab side indentations for the installation of tablet catcher facilities although these were never actually required. None of the Class 3 subdivision was ever fitted with boilers and they were, therefore, rarely seen on passenger workings north of the border.

There were sufficient spare Class 25s by the end of 1971 to oust the last medium power diesel-hydraulics from West of England local services, although they were never popular with the crews. The Western Region's patience with the survivors of the North British Class 22 'D63XX' fleet had finally run out, and the Sulzer invasion which had hit South Wales a couple of years earlier, spread to Cornwall on 30 July when D5180 ran light to St Blazey for inspection. Three weeks later it was joined by D5179. After crew training at Laira and St Blazey with D5180 and D5181 from Ebbw Junction, Newport, the first actual reallocation was that of D7657 to Laira with effect from October 1971.

The class's use as replacements for withdrawn types on other regions saw some remarkable transfers. None was more interesting than that of D5246 (25.096) which left Toton in May 1973 and by the time it was withdrawn in October 1977 had been allocated to (in order): Eastfield, Haymarket, Bescot, Bristol, Laira, Haymarket, Inverness, Eastfield, Toton and finally back to Eastfield. It then remained in Scotland and was scrapped at Glasgow works.

Decline

The first Class 25 withdrawal was that of D5278 which was involved in a head-on single line collision near Great Rocks in Derbyshire during May 1971. It was withdrawn that month and later moved to Peak Forest where a local scrap merchant cut it up during October of that year. The second member of the class to go was D7605 on 16 December 1971 when it too was in collision, this time with a pair of Toton-based Class 20s, whilst working the 06.30 Liverpool Lime Street-Nottingham PCD parcels.

1980 saw the final transfer and withdrawal of the

remaining Western Region Class 25s. The dual-braked locomotives were transferred to the Midland Region together with 25.080, being recently overhauled and boiler fitted. The others (25.052/223/225) were all due for classified works overhaul, and as the expenditure was not authorised they were sent to Swindon to be cut up.

Although the decline of the Class 25 fleet continues, its pace has been greatly reduced over the past few months, chiefly because most of the vacuum-braked members have already been condemned, and also because of a slight upturn in the economy. There is also a lack of suitable replacement locomotives from elsewhere. No classified repairs have been carried out on the class since 25.278 was released from a general overhaul in Derby works during January 1981. In consequence, although some unclassified repairs have been authorised to the traction motors of the dual braked members of the class at Derby, their availability has without doubt suffered. In the past few months four previously condemned Class 25s have been reinstated to traffic, namely 25.237 and 25.257 at Crewe, 25.316 at Longsight and 25.322 (named *Tamworth Castle*) at Bescot, and all after depot attention.

Three members of the class were converted to unpowered 'Ethel' ETH units for use behind Class 37 locomotives on the West Highland line in Scotland, but unfortunately have not been very successful. However, their days appear to be numbered as the first Class 37 (37.268) entered Crewe works for ETH conversion in July 1984. The three locomotives involved were previously numbered 25.305 (Ethel 2, ADB97251), 25.310 (Ethel 1, ADB97250) and 25.314 (Ethel 3, ADB97252); all are now allocated to Eastfield for maintenance. The specifications, allocations and fitment modifications of the remaining class members by mid-March 1985 were as follows:

Weight: 71-76 tons
Brake force: 38 tons
Engine: Sulzer 6LDA28B of 930kW (1,250hp) at 750rpm
Traction motors: AEI 253AY axle hung
Wheel dia: 1,143mm (3ft 9in)
Power at rail: 708kW (949hp)
Max TE: 200kN (45,000lb/ft)
Cont TE: 93kN (20,800lb/ft), at 17.1mph
Max speed: 90mph
MW: Blue star
RA 5

I = boiler fitted but isolated.

Engine	*Allocation*	*DB*	*SH*	*Engine*	*Allocation*	*DB*	*SH*
25.032	CD	*		25.224	CD		*
25.034	BS	*	*	25.226	CD	*	I
25.035	CD	*	*	25.229	CD	*	I
25.037	CD	*	I	25.230	CD	*	I
25.042	CD		*	25.231	CD	*	I
25.044	KD	*	*	25.235	CD	*	*
25.048	BS	*	*	25.237	CD	*	I
25.051	BS	*	*	25.244	CD	*	I
25.054	CD	*	I	25.245	CD	*	*
25.057	LO	*	*	25.249	CD	*	
25.058	BS	*	*	25.254	CD	*	
25.059	CD	*	I	25.256	CD	*	
25.060	CD	*	*	25.257	CD	*	
25.064	CD	*	I	25.259	BS	*	
25.072	CD	*	I	25.262	BS	*	
25.078	CD	*	I	25.265	CD	*	
25.080	CD		*	25.266	CD	*	
25.089	CD	*		25.268	CD	*	
25.095	BS	*		25.269	BS	*	
25.109	CD	*		25.276	BS	*	
25.119	CD			25.278	KD	*	
25.145	BS	*		25.279	CD	*	
25.154	BS	*		25.282	BS	*	
25.173	CD	*		25.283	CD	*	
25.175	CD	*		25.285	CD	*	
25.176	KD	*		25.286	CD	*	
25.178	CD	*		25.287	CD	*	
25.181	CD	*		25.288	CD	*	
25.189	CD	*		25.296	CD	*	
25.190	CD	*		25.297	CD	*	
25.191	KD	*		25.298	CD	*	
25.192	CD	*		25.300	CD	*	
25.194	CD	*		25.302	CD		
25.195	CD			25.303	CD	*	
25.196	KD	*		25.307	KD	*	
25.198	KD	*		25.309	KD	*	
25.199	KD	*		25.313	BS	*	
25.200	KD	*		25.315	CD	*	
25.201	KD	*		25.316	LO	*	
25.202	KD	*		25.321	LO	*	
25.205	BS	*		25.322	BS	*	
25.206	CD	*		25.323	CD	*	
25.209	BS	*		25.324	LO	*	
25.210	CD	*		25.325	BS	*	
25.211	BS	*					
25.212	CD	*					
25.213	CD	*		Total: 91 (11/3/85)			

Right: One of Laira TMD's original batch of Class 25s, No 7575 (renumbered 25.225), shunts milk tanks at Hemyock on 8 April 1972. It had just arrived with the 14.28 trip from Exeter New Yard which on this occasion conveyed members of the LCGB's Bath branch in two fitted brake vans — hence the smart headboard! It is interesting that 25.225 was one of only three out of all the Western Region's allocation of '25s' to remain on the Western Region throughout the rest of its working life.
G. R. Hounsell

Above: A study of Class 25/0 No 5174, latterly 25.024, whilst allocated to Tinsley TMD. It was seen here between turns of duty at Frodingham fuel point on 16 July 1973. The shot clearly shows the body side grilles, bogies, battery boxes and fuel tanks, which were all very similar to the later Class 24/1s.

Top: No 7513 heads out of Gloucester with a once familiar sight — an empty raft of mineral wagons destined for the Midlands — after a short stop for crew relief. The shot, taken on a February morning in 1971, is never likely to be repeated as freights on Sundays, even specials these days, are exceedingly rare, and faster, air-braked wagons are now in use in preference to the 35mph MCVs and MCOs depicted.

Above: Although already fitted with dual brakes, Wigan Springs Branch's Class 25/3 No 7635 was still in two-tone green livery when photographed in Gloucester Central station during April 1972. It was working a local Sunday ballast train. Like the livery, the Toad brake van behind the locomotive is now a thing of the past.

Below: In September 1973 the first Class 25 was released from BREL's Derby works after classified repairs, carrying the new TOPS computerised numbering system namely 25.208. Here it is seen on 10 September working in multiple with fellow class member No 5248 after successfully completing its ex-works test run to Leicester the day before.

Bottom: An 'Ethel' unit No 97251 (once 25.305) stands at Oban shortly after being released from Aberdeen Ferryhill where it underwent conversion.

Variations on a theme

Officially the Class 25 can be divided into four main categories: 25/0, 25/1, 25/2 and 25/3. Within these subdivisions there is a wealth of variety in liveries, position of vents and other modifications such as whether fitted with boilers, dual brakes, snow ploughs or tablet catcher recesses.

Class 25/0

Originally numbered D5151 to D5175 (25.001-25) this now extinct subdivision was externally not dissimilar to the last batch of Class 24s, being fitted with a headcode panel above the cab windows but no roof-mounted air warning horns. None of them were fitted with train heating boilers, but all were vacuum-braked and Darlington-built.

Class 25/1

Once again this batch of locomotives were all Darlington-built and carried the numbers D5176 to D5232 (25.026-82). All except four (5179-82), were boiler-fitted, and a large number (particularly those allocated to the Scottish region), were eventually fitted with dual brakes and snow plough brackets.

Class 25/2

At the end of 1963 a major design change took place in the Class 25 building programme, when a new bodyside and cab configuration was introduced. The previous mass of bodyside grilles was replaced by a line of vents above cant rail height. Only two grilles were left on the actual bodyside, one beside the boiler cubicle, and the other in the radiator compartment. On the front end the centre gangway doors gave way to three full sized cab windows, and in addition the internal layout of the cab was also greatly changed. By now several works were building the locomotives at the same time. This resulted in an anomaly in the numbering system. Consequentially the Class 25/2 subdivision falls into two types: D5233-5299 (25.083-25.149) and D7500-7567 (25.150-25.217) were built to the new specification; D7568-7597

Below: No 25.001 was photographed at Swindon works after it had arrived with three fellow condemned members of the class on 2 November 1980. The print shows the locomotive after a classified repair at Glasgow works with its associated Scottish Region-style livery (although it still carries the conventional sized loco number).

(25.218-25.247) were built to the old style at Darlington.

Class 25/3

None of the 25/3 subdivision Nos D7598-D7677 (25.248-25.327) were ever fitted with any type of train heating facility, although several have now been converted into 'Ethel' units to provide the ETH power on the West Highland line in connection with the introduction of Mk III sleepers on the route. As was the case with all Crewe works overhauled Class 25s, the number was affixed to the body side rather than below the cab windows, even on the non-tablet catcher specimens, together with a considerably larger than normal BR insignia.

Below: A spring day in 1975 saw 25.013, still allocated to Tinsley, stabled at Warrington Arpley. The locomotive was carrying the standard Derby-style livery and had not received any classified works attention since renumbering. (See also fig 1.)

Bottom: A vacuum-braked member of the class, No 25.056, is seen stabled on Thornaby TMD in the standard LMR Derby-style livery, shortly before being condemned.

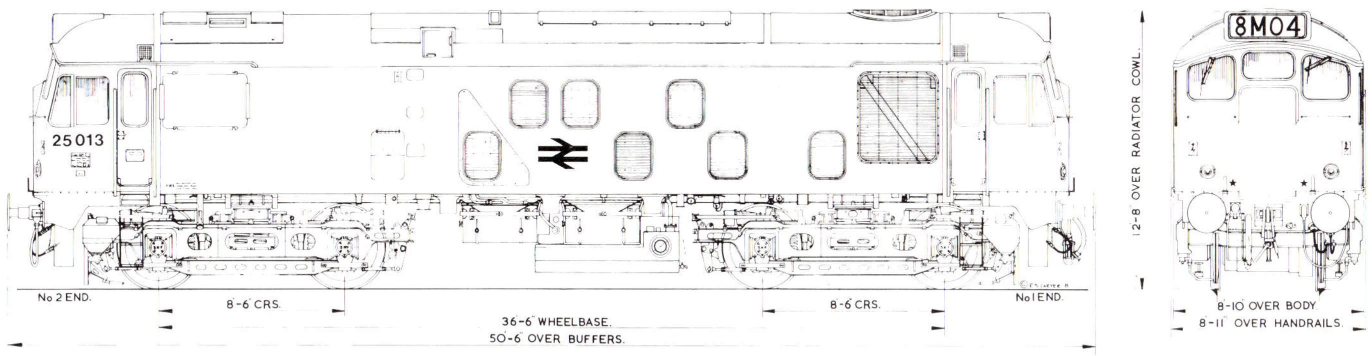

Fig 1 Class 25/0.

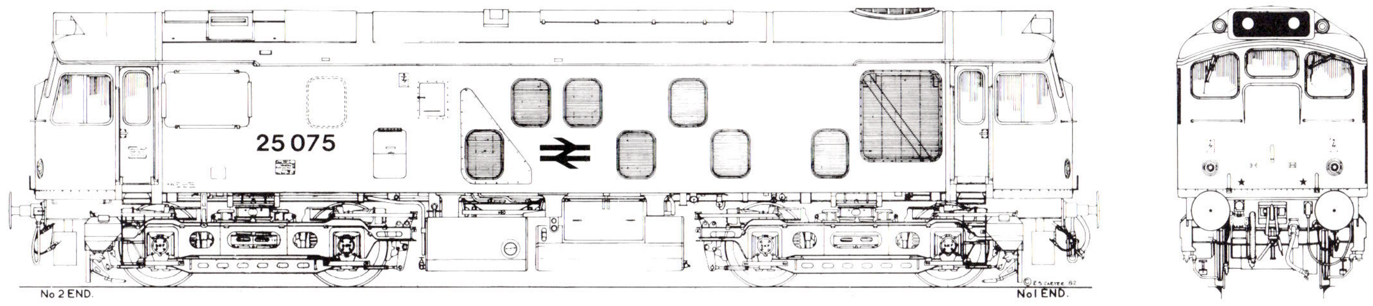

Fig 2 Class 25/1.

Above: One of the last batch of Class 25 locomotives to be transferred from the London Midland Region to the Scottish Region at the end of the 1970s, No 25.064 was fitted with dual brakes in Glasgow works, shortly after arrival.

Below: Only three Class 25/1s which were given classified works overhauls at Glasgow after transfer from the London Midland Region did not receive dual brakes. However, the three (25.062, 25.066, 25.075) did have the distinction of being given extra-large body side numbers. (See also fig 2.)

Above: Only five new style Class 25s, all members of the '25/2' subdivision, were ever built with boilers. These were D5233-5237 (25.083-87) and had all been transferred to the Scottish Region by the end of the 1970s. None were ever dual-braked even though all bar 25.087 were given a second classified works overhaul and large numbers whilst north of the border. The additional boiler water tank is clearly visible under the body, between the bogies, on this picture of 25.085.

Below: A study of 25.110, a vacuum-braked member of the Class 25/2 subdivision, built to the new design but without a boiler.

Fig 3 Class 25/2.

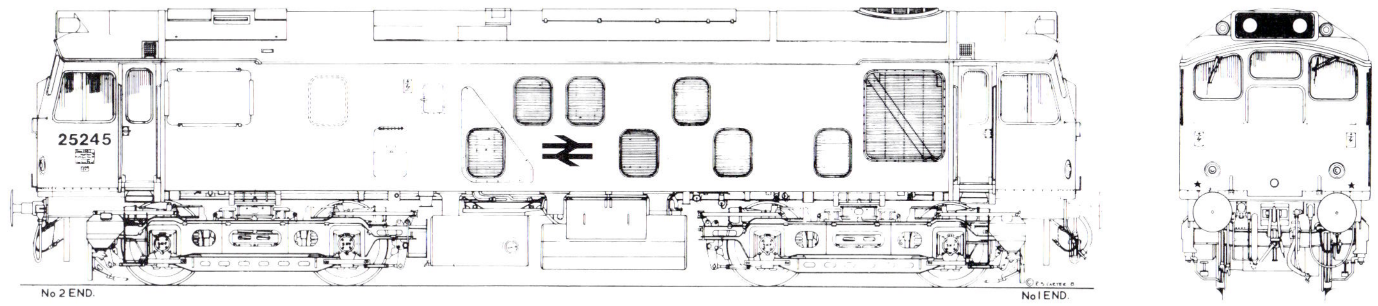

Fig 4 Class 25/3.

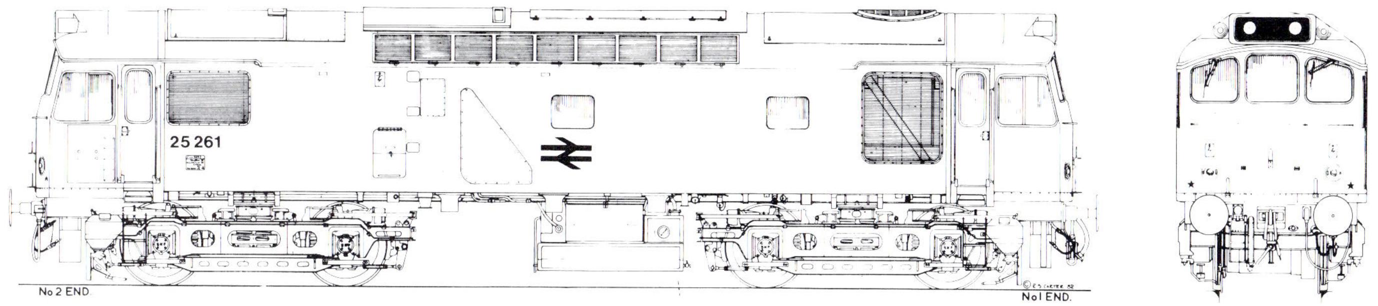

Above: No 25.209 was one of the last batch of Class 25/2 locomotives allocated to the LMR to be dual-brake fitted at its last Derby works classified overhaul. About half of the subdivision was eventually dealt with in this manner before the classified shopping programme was finished.

Below: When 25.245 entered traffic in 1964, Darlington works was in the process of building its last two Class 25s, all of them having been built to the old multi-grille design. Eventually, Darlington's Class 25 batch contained no less than 24 dual-braked members out of a possible total of 30, and until recent years all (with the exception of 25.242), retained fully operational steam heat boilers. (See also fig 3.)

No 25.245, pictured at the back of its home maintenance depot, Crewe, is one of a select band which can claim to have regularly hauled royal trains. The black disc on the cab front indicates where a radio telephone wire was passed to enable the driver and guard to keep in touch during such occasions.

Above left and left: Both 25.261 and 25.267 were last overhauled at Crewe during the mid-1970s and as such were never considered for dual braking. They are both members of a small batch of Class 25/3s fitted with cab side indentations for use on the Scottish Region's tablet block sections of line. It is interesting to note that when the photograph was taken of 25.261, it had lost its grille cover from just behind the leading door. (See also fig 4.)

Below: A standard Class 25/3 livery is shown on 25.282 which is fitted with dual brakes, and was last overhauled during May 1978 at Derby.

Double-headed workings

All Class 25 locomotives were fitted with blue star multiple working equipment when built. This enables two members of the class to work together on a train, but be operated by a single driver situated in the leading cab. This type of operation is called 'multiple working.' When two locomotives not so fitted are driven by two drivers it is known as 'tandem working'. When a train is worked by two locomotives in multiple, the total weight they can move is the same as that of the two individual locomotives. If, however, the locomotives are working in tandem, then the weight they can haul is only equivalent to the applicable load of the largest locomotive plus half the smaller one's maximum loading. One small variation is the fact that when a Class 25/3 is in multiple with any other Class 25 subdivision the permitted loading must be reduced by 25% because of problems that have been experienced with the traction motors. The virtue of being able to work locomotives of the same class in multiple is illustrated by the fact that two Class 25s, although only having a combined horsepower of 2,500, can haul larger loads over most routes than a Class 47 with its 2,580hp. Obviously the total weight distribution and wheel arrangements have a bearing on this aspect too.

Below: A pair of ex-Scottish Type 2s, Nos 25.075 and 25.086 (both vacuum-braked and boiler-fitted), pass Crewe North Stafford Junction with 8F21 12.40 SX COY Oakamoor to Springs Branch freight on 11 May 1982. The service is conveying high quality sand for use in the production of glass at Ravenhead by Pilkingtons. *P. Kynaston*

Above: Nos 25.116 and 25.160 trundle through Alsager in Stoke-on-Trent with a special Corby to Birkenhead freight, conveying iron ore pellets during March 1977.

Below: By mid-morning on 3 August 1982, 25.287 and 25.250 were ready to leave Holditch colliery sidings with Crewe No 52 trip. On their way back to Basford Hall sorting sidings they had to run round the fully fitted service at Apedale Junction and then rejoin the West Coast main line by means of Madeley chord. *P. Kynaston*

Above: A pair of Springs Branch dual-braked Class 25/3s many miles from home. Nos 25.285 and 25.289 stand on the through road at Newton Abbot with a Gulf Oil service from Ellesmere Port to Heathfield, on the former Moreton Hampstead branch. *R. W. Penny*

Below: The last two Beyer Peacock-built Class 25/3s, Nos 25.308 and 25.309, seem to be making light work of this rake of empty Bitumen tanks from Cranmore in Somerset to Ellesmere Port. *R. W. Penny*

Below: Wrenbury, between Nantwich and Whitchurch, makes a lovely setting for this shot of 25.095 and 25.076 at the head of 6V32, the 14.56 Bitumen service from Ellesmere Port to Exeter City Basin, on 15 June 1983.
P. Kynaston

Bottom: Taking a turn normally booked for a Class 47, 25.154 and 25.221 are seen here with 6E40, the 15.40 (Sun) Ince and Elton to Whitemoor UKF service during September 1981.

Top: Class 25/2 No 25.088 and 25/3 No 25.314, both now withdrawn, head across Salop Goods Junction on the independent lines at Crewe, on 25 May 1977, whilst working 4F53 — the 14.34 SX COY Forders Sidings to Garston (via Longsight, Manchester), Fletliner brick service.

Above: No 25.270 and 25.107 stand in Alston sidings with the stock from a Nelson-Cheltenham charter service.

Below: On 26 August 1979, 25.273 and 25.298 could be found on the siding beside Barmouth fire station with the stock of an Adex from Melton Mowbray.

Bottom: On the same day the Sunday summer dated service train to Euston stood behind 25.032 and 25.320 in Barmouth station. A few months after the photograph was taken the nearby Barmouth bridge was closed to all rail traffic whilst bridge repair costs were assessed. A marine worm called the Torado was found to have eaten its way into all of the wooden supports, and it was decided that after certain repairs, a DMU service only would be reintroduced to Barmouth and Pwllheli.

Above: The 10.50 relief from Aberdeen to King's Cross approaching Haymarket station at a leisurely pace behind 25.085 and 25.023 during August 1975. The pair worked the train to Newcastle, where they were replaced by a single Class 55 locomotive.

Below: The good old days! A Paignton-Paddington summer Saturday holiday relief heads past Aller Junction near Newton Abbot, behind Midland Region '25/3s' Nos 25.265 and 25.264. *R. W. Penny*

The Cambrian line in central Wales is one of the few Class 25 turn strongholds. On 23 July 1983, 25.250 and 25.296 were seen climbing the bank at Talerddig with the 14.00 Aberystwyth to Shrewsbury service. *R. A. Lissenden*

Left: No 25.285 found it impossible to restart on 16 April 1980 after coming to a stand at signals protecting New Mills South Junction with a rake of empty limestone hoppers. After a short delay the engine and train were hauled to Tunstead by No 47.306 which had come light from Guide Bridge. Later the failed engine was dragged to Buxton for attention. *Noel Johnston*

Below: Here, the boot is on the other foot! 25.088 comes to the rescue of 40.026 after it had failed somewhere on route from Northwich. The Tunstead-bound limestone empties are seen making slow progress up the 1 in 90 climb to Chinley station on 15 July 1980. *Noel Johnston*

On shed and under maintenance

For the purpose of maintaining locomotives in general on British Rail, and in an effort to prevent failures in traffic, all locomotives are allocated to a home maintenance depot. From time to time this allocation is altered because of variations in traffic flows, etc, both Regionally and inter-Regionally. At these depots locomotives undergo regular routine maintenance, which falls into a number of categories. Every time a locomotive enters a depot for fuel it is serviced, or given a daily examination. In addition to this, every 55 hours of actual running time it undergoes an 'A' examination, which normally takes several hours to complete, depending on how much work is found to be needed. Once a locomotive becomes due its fifth 'A' examination (ie after 275 hours of running), it is given a 'B' examination, which is a more thorough one than the 'A'. In addition to the above maintenance, locomotives also receive 'C', 'D' and 'E' examinations at traction maintenance depots (TMDs), and both classified and unclassified works overhauls from time to time.

Again on 14 February 1981, Class 25/2s Nos 25.161 and 25.151 rest side by side at Cockshute holding sidings, before being called for their next turns of duty.

Below: Although there are 15 locomotives depicted in this general shot of Stoke Cockshute depot taken on 14 February 1981, there are no fuelling or maintenance facilities at this location. The locomotives have to make regular trips to Crewe TMD for fuel, coolant, and minor repairs, or to their home maintenance depots for larger repairs. Of the 15 'on shed' only six are Class 25s — Nos 25.151, 25.306, 25.161, 25.139, 25.258 and 25.148.

Bottom: No 25.219 has its batteries recharged inside Crewe TMD whilst standing beside 47.454.

Top: To enable access to the engine compartment of 25.159 the triangular-shaped body side cover has been removed. The locomotive was undergoing a 'B' examination on 10 October 1979 inside Crewe TMD. Alongside, 25.073 was receiving attention to its train heat boiler.

Above: Fresh from royal train duties, with the associated 'bulling up' of its paintwork, 25.259 stands buffered up to 25.149 on Crewe holding sidings during September 1980.

Left: No 25.316 (incidentally one of several locomotives to be reinstated during 1984) was photographed back in 1977 receiving attention inside Crewe TMD. At the back (behind the Class 47) with the modified headcode panel was 25.063. This engine has now been withdrawn.

Right: After being released off maintenance at Buxton, 25.172 passed the time of day stabled with the DMUs, behind the station, in the carriage sidings.

Below: The sun catches the sides of 25.289 and 25.264 as they stand stabled beside 47.328 on Nuneaton holding sidings, during May 1979.

Above: An immaculate 25.058, fresh from a Derby works classified overhaul and with splendid new paintwork, poses for the camera on Newton Abbot holding sidings. *R. W. Penny*

Below: During the middle of 1973, the Scottish Region despatched D5349 to Derby works for fire damage attention. Here it is seen on 10 September 1973 inside the works, beside 7545 which had itself returned for rectification.

Light movements

One of the less productive aspects of railway operating is the light mileage certain diagrams entail to move a locomotive between locations for its next turn of duty. In addition to diagrammed moves, it is also necessary to move locomotives for maintenance reasons, ie for examinations, repairs or even ultrasonic axle tests, on an ad hoc basis.

Below: On 17 February 1980, the Camp Hill bank engine (in the shape of 25.290) took a well earned rest after assisting a Didcot-bound MGR service past Saltley TMD. The MGR service needed assistance in restarting after it had stopped for a crew change at Landor Street Junction.

Bottom: En route from March TMD to Norwood Yard, 25.312 has left the engine spur at Whitemoor Junction, in readiness to work a freight to Toton down the now disused GE-GN joint line; October 1981.

A well travelled Class 25/2, No 25.092 heads south across the viaduct at Killiecrankie during July 1975, whilst making its way from Inverness to Perth, having assisted with ballast workings in the area.

Below: No 25.154 passes the ground frame at Cheltenham High Street sidings during August 1982 whilst running light from Worcester to Gloucester.

Bottom: After running light from Toton, 25.253 idles quietly away on one of the avoiding lines in Leicester station whilst waiting for the all clear to run on to the adjacent depot, 31 August 1982. *P. A. Biggs*

Below: Nos 25.327 and 25.287 hurry through Alsager station during March 1977 on their way from Cockshute holding sidings to Crewe for fuel and water, only to return an hour or so later for their next booked workings at Stoke.

Bottom: A trio of vacuum-braked Class 25/2s head south through Harpenden en route from Leicester to Cricklewood on 23 June 1979. They are 25.125, 25.167 and 25.187, all long since withdrawn. *R. A. Lissenden*

Freight services

By far and away the most useful and prolific work performed by the Class 25s over the years has been in the freight field. They have regularly worked everything from the humble local trip to the largest of company trains. They usually work the latter in pairs and have been quite at home on all manner of freight work, as I hope the following photographs will show.

Below: Before being dual-braked during its last works classified overhaul during 1977, 25.323 is seen approaching Cheadle (Cheshire Lines Committee), with a loaded freight from Tunstead quarry to Northwich, conveying hoppers of limestone.
Noel Johnston

Again with a loaded service, 25.191 (fitted with dual brakes and miniature snow ploughs) is seen approaching Hale on the former CLC line from Altrincham to Chester on 8 September 1978. *Noel Johnston*

Top: No 25.217 heads through Peak Forest with a rake of empty limestone hoppers.

Above: On 21 June 1983, 25.115 was captured on film powering up the bank into Chinley with the 6H42 08.21 Oakleigh to Peak Forest sidings ICI service. *P. Kynaston*

Below: The bogie limestone hoppers seen behind 25.274 on 19 April 1980 have been a familiar sight in the Peak District for many years and date back to the 1950s. This service is seen on the former Midland Railway line near Chapel-en-le-Frith and was about to pass under the former LNWR Stockport-Buxton branch, whilst en route from Oakleigh to Great Rocks. *Noel Johnston*

Bottom: The last Class 25 to receive any kind of classified works overhaul, 25.278 shunts a raft of empty stone flat-bottomed wagons into the quarry sidings just to the north of Peak Forest yard, on 20 April 1982. *Noel Johnston*

Above: On 30 March 1977, 25.088 passed Faulders sidings ground frame near Georges Road on the now disused line from Cheadle Junction and Woodley Junction, with a train of cement presflos. The ground on which the photographer stood to take the shot was formerly a marshalling yard and is now part of the M63 Motorway. *Noel Johnston*

Top: On the downhill stretch between New Mills and Marple 25.056 is seen passing through Strines station on 26 May 1977 with a mixed freight trip bound for Dewsnap sidings near Guide Bridge. *Noel Johnston*

No 25.285 passes Apthorne Junction near Woodley on 27 July 1976 with a freight conveying two empty car transporters, four ferry type vans, and sandwiched between, a couple of chlorine tanks destined for the Murgatroid sidings at Sandbach. The other wagons were, in fact, doubling up as barrier vehicles because loaded or empty chlorine tanks, unless purged, are classified as dangerous goods when conveyed by rail. The line to the left of the picture is now closed but at one time connected with the Woodhead electrified route at Godley Junction. *Noel Johnston*

Top: Four vacuum-braked wagons of grain for export approach Helsby behind 25.123 on 22 May 1982, on their way to Birkenhead docks. *P. Kynaston*

Above: Although usually diagrammed for larger Type 4 locomotives, Class 25s are often used as substitutes on Speedlink freights if the traffic is light. Here, 25.256 stands at the top of the chord from Salop Goods Junction to Gresty Lane Junction at Crewe, with the 6V92 Garston-Severn Tunnel Junction Bristol yard air-braked network service during August 1981.

Top: No 25.303 is seen shortly after emerging from under the West Coast main line with a Basford Hall sorting sidings middle, Crewe, to Cockshute yard, Stoke, local mixed trip.

Above: A rake of mineral empties head up the independent lines from Crewe on 6 February 1979, behind 25.215. They are running as 8L27 an 11.00 special from Garston to Washwood Heath, ready for reloading at Midland collieries.

Below: Emerging slowly out of Northgate tunnel at Chester on 19 July 1983 comes 25.032 heading for the station with two brake vans from Mold Junction.
P. A. Biggs

Bottom: On 27 April 1984, behind 25.154, the 7L82 12.20 SX COY Leekbrook-Witton Tarmac roadstone freight leaves Bescot up sidings after a brief lay over. At Witton (on the outskirts of Birmingham), there is a council owned aggregates terminal from where the stone is distributed generally (as opposed to being used for any one specific project). *P. Kynaston*

No 25.117 runs under Croes Newydd signal quadrant and passes through the level crossing at Wrexham, whilst heading for Croes Newydd yard on 26 July 1982, with a small trip from Mostyn Docks, Deeside. It is interesting to note the repairs being carried out (below the-right hand side of the signal) to the bridge which carries the line over the Wrexham General-Bidston line.
P. A. Biggs

Top: 25.120 rattles across Horton Road level crossing at Gloucester with 8V63 — the 11.05 SX Tinsley Sheffield to Severn Tunnel Junction freight on 29 June 1976.

Above: Whilst allocated to Cardiff Canton TMD, 7521 was photographed working a special Cardiff tidal sidings to Washwood Heath, Birmingham freight of empty mineral wagons to Gloucester, during February 1971. It is interesting to note that although this locomotive was never fitted with a train heating boiler it was piped and fitted with a steam hose so that it could work in multiple with a boiler-fitted member of the class on passenger services during the winter months.

Left: Heading through the Cotswolds in August 1984, 25.136 works a Toton-Westbury mixed freight through a location to the south of Cheltenham. Such a variety of wagons on one train is now, sadly, a thing of the past.

Right: In the early morning light of 26 March 1982 No 25.201 powers towards Wichnor Junction with a rake of MGR hoppers, released off programmed maintenance at Burton-on-Trent, bound for Bescot yard. *P. Kynaston*

Below right: The Molex Drain train is seen passing through Toton on 22 May 1983 behind 25.048. It consists of a bogie tank wagon and two four-wheeled tanks with a brake van at each end. The brake vans double up as barrier wagons. *G. Grafton*

Below: A Bescot to Gloucester freight in the capable hands of 25.194 approaches Brockhampton level crossing near Ashchurch during May 1979.

Above: A crisp shot of 25.297 as it passes Benneley colliery with an up Tinsley to Toton service, conveying mainly household coal. At one time this type of freight was regularly to be seen on the Erewash Valley route, although the introduction of air-braked, high capacity wagons has now reduced their frequency considerably. The disused viaduct in the background once carried the GN line from Derby to Grantham, Peterborough and eventually on to King's Cross. Photograph 16 April 1982. *P. Kynaston*

Below: No 25.312 heads through Cossington on the evening of 24 February 1982 with a train of sheeted gypsum, conveyed in unfitted mineral wagons.
P. Kynaston

Top: Nottingham station clock tower provides an interesting backcloth for this photograph of 25.286 as it hauls a local trip from Grantham yard to the permanent way depot at Mansfield Junction on 30 October 1978.
P. Kynaston

Above: Class 25/1 No 25.059 pulls a southbound train of four-wheeled oil tank wagons through Clay Mills to the north of Burton-on-Trent on 21 July 1983. *C. J. Tuffs*

Left: No 25.070 prepares to leave Warrington Walton old junction yard with a Croes Newydd-bound mixed freight on 26 August 1980. The vacuum-braked Presflo wagons marshalled behind the engine were destined for Penyffordd, and had originated at Gunnie on the Scottish Region.

Below: On 9 September 1971, shortly after its transfer from the Eastern Region's depot at Leeds Holbeck to the LMR's Toton, 7572 (later 25.222) rests in Cockshute yard at Stoke with a Bescot-bound 8L77 special mixed freight.

Right: No 25.218 passes through Shipley with a special out of gauge freight from Embsey to Codmoor Park on Thursday 2 June 1983, conveying two ex-MSJ&A electric coaches. *J. Fozard*

Below right: A Dringhouses yard to York yard north trip is seen between these two locations behind 25.278 on 25 July 1978. *P. Kynaston*

Whilst allocated to Laira, and before the total introduction of Class 37s to cover all china clay workings in the St Blazey area, 25.206 arrives at Lostwithiel with an early morning loaded service from St Austell. After shunting, and once the engine had run round its wagons, the train eventually left for Fowey Harbour on 2 August 1979. *P. Kynaston*

On 10 August 1982 (whilst allocated to the Scottish Region) 25.059 was utilised to shunt locomotive fuel tanks on to the stabling point at Perth, from the north end of the station. It had arrived with the tanks earlier that day from Millerhill yard. *P. Kynaston*

Passenger and parcels trains

Over the years Class 25s have appeared on many small formation Class 1 and 2 passenger and parcel services. They are still regularly used in pairs during the summer months on the Cambrian line from Wolverhampton to Aberystwyth, because of route availability problems with larger locomotives. In addition, they occasionally substitute on the Norwich/Cambridge to Birmingham services, for Class 31/4 failures. They are also often to be found hauling failed DMUs all over the Midland Region, where they are all now based. Stock movements in and out of Manchester Piccadilly and Liverpool Lime Street stations are often diagrammed to Class 25 traction, as are certain Preston-Blackpool feeder services. Until their mass transfer from Cricklewood and subsequent replacement by heavier Class 31 locomotives, '25s' were often hauling dead EMUs and electric locomotives with their pantographs lowered, under the wires on the West Coast main line between Nuneaton and Euston. This would happen particularly on Sundays when engineering work required the overhead line equipment to be isolated at various points.

Crewe diesel depot could boast the last diagrammed work for boiler-fitted Class 25s, because their locomotives worked the Crewe to Cardiff services solidly before the introduction of ETH-fitted Class 33s in May 1981. Although there are still 15 boiler-fitted locomotives in service, the only jobs they now perform to any great extent, are the pre-heating of stock during the winter months and at night-time. They also work specials, including engineer's saloons.

The following photographs depict some of the past and present turns of duty which Class 25 traction has been allocated over the years.

Below: During the long hot summer of 1976, DMU availability on the Western Region reached an all time low. Here, deputising for one such failure, the 12.45 Cardiff-Weston-super-Mare service passed Bedminster, behind 25.137.

No 25.051 hauls AM10 EMU No 058 out of Rugby on Sunday 16 September 1979, whilst working the 2A24 11.38 service to Euston. On this particular Sunday the road between Northampton and Hanslope Junction was blocked and the OLE switched off between Rugby and Bletchley.

Above: No 25.037 enters Bristol Temple Meads station, after a heavy check at the east signal gantry, with a Cardiff to Taunton local service during March 1975. The boiler was working well on this occasion, as evidenced by the amount of steam escaping from behind the coaches.

Below: A grimy 25.059 drifts down Filton Bank towards Lawrence Hill station on the relief lines, with another DMU substitution during the summer of 1976.

Above: No 25.052 stands in Bristol Temple Meads shortly after arriving with a failed cross-country DMU. This had been running in the path of the delayed 1V56 00.05 Glasgow and Edinburgh to Bristol sleeper which itself had sustained electric locomotive failure at Crewe on the Midland Region and was reported some 120 minutes late as a result.

Below: After a short stay of only a few days in the Motorail platform at Bristol, 25.294 leaves the east end of the station with the BR safety publicity train during September 1976.

No 25.063 motors through Pontrilas with the 10.00 Crewe-Cardiff in February 1975.

Above: No 25.224 was once a familiar sight in Wales, and is here captured in Newport station after arriving with the 1V01 06.00 Crewe-Cardiff service on 29 April 1980.
P. Kynaston

Below: No 25.151 prepares to depart from Shrewsbury station on 4 August 1979 whilst working the 4V20 15.10 MSX Manchester Piccadilly-Bristol Temple Meads parcel service. *P. Kynaston*

On 18 April 1981 No 25.060 hurries past pleasant surroundings to the south of Abergavenny with the 1V05 12.25 Crewe-Cardiff. The following month the service was transferred to Class 33 haulage in line with a move to utilise ETH traction on passenger trains wherever possible.
R. A. Lissenden

Above: Track recording coach DW139 is seen marshalled behind 25.184 as they leave Shrewsbury en route for Cardiff on 22 June 1983 with an empty stock service. *G. Grafton*

Below: Conveying three GUVs, two BGs and a BSK, 25.228 hurries towards Whitchurch, Salop with 4V20 — the 15.10 MSX Manchester Piccadilly-Bristol Temple Meads parcels, on 12 August 1983. *P. Kynaston*

Running approximately 40 minutes late, 25.268 hurries the 11.15 Norwich-Birmingham away from Melton Mowbray after replacing a defective Class 31/4 at March on 9 June 1983. *R. A. Lissenden*

Right: No 25.262 is seen to the north of Syston Junction near Leicester with the 08.38 service to Skegness on 6 August 1983. On arrival at Nottingham the locomotive became a failure and was replaced by 45.113. *R. A. Lissenden*

Below: The weekday 5P35 Willesden carriage sidings to Derby Etches Park empty carriage stock service is seen at Burbage Common cutting near Hinckley behind 25.262 on 30 March 1983. Amongst the 14 vehicles forming the train was Cricklewood-based Class 127 DMU power car No M51616. *P. A. Biggs*

Right: Narborough station forms the backcloth as 25.037 is seen hauling the daily ECS from Willesden Sudbury sidings to Derby Litchurch Lane works on 26 August 1983. The Class 25 had only worked the train from Nuneaton Trent Valley station, having taken over from an AC electric locomotive some 30 minutes earlier. *P. A. Biggs*

Right: No 25.157 shunts a failed Crewe-Lincoln DMU service out of Stoke-on-Trent station on 15 March 1978.

Below: 1V03, the 10.00 Crewe-Cardiff service, crosses Crewe South Junction shortly after departure, during May 1978, behind 25.159.

Left: On the evening of 24 February 1977, 25.056 stands in Crewe station with a parcels service which it had previously worked in from Bangor. It awaits the go ahead to propel the empty vans into up hill sidings (now closed), so that they could be remarshalled into other forward services.

Below: No 25.224 at Helsby on 10 May 1982 with an inspection special. *P. Kynaston*

Left: Until recently summer Saturdays saw Class 25s as regular visitors to the north Wales coast on passenger services. Here, on 22 May 1982, 25.130 returns to Manchester Victoria with the 11.49 from Bangor, and is seen passing Sandy Croft signalbox between Chester and Shotton. *P. A. Biggs*

Below: Class 25s Nos 25.084 and 25.048 are seen passing Hucknell Pit on the freight only line from Radford Junction to Annesley colliery with a railtour on 22 April 1983. *G. Grafton*

Above: The 12.00 Scarborough-Liverpool Lime Street passes Marsden on 24 July 1982 behind 25.158. *R. A. Lissenden*

Below: With a number of 'haulage bashers' evident in the first coach, 25.300 crosses Ravensthorpe Junction on 24 July 1982 with the 08.40 summer Saturday Manchester-Scarborough service. *R. A. Lissenden*

Top: Manchester Victoria station pilot (vacuum-braked Class 25 No 25.139) busies itself shunting a parcels van towards West Junction on 21 August 1982.
Noel Johnston

Above: No 25.228 passes Eastfield depot with a motley rake of vans forming an Edinburgh-Glasgow parcels service on 27 April 1975.

Above: The 11.04 Perth-Edinburgh service stands ready to depart on 29 July 1978, behind 25.008 (long since withdrawn). The passengers seen joining the middle coaches of the train had just arrived on a late running Inverness-Glasgow Queen Street service hauled by two Class 26 locomotives.

Below: No 25.108 crosses the viaduct to the north of Rannoch station on the West Highland line, whilst working 1T45 — the 12.50 Mallaig-Glasgow Queen Street (via Fort William) service — on 31 July 1978.

Below: No 25.228 arrives at Largs with a Scottish Railway Preservation Society special from Fife, including a number of preserved coaches, on 21 May 1977. At Largs passengers were able to join Wirral Railway Circle members from Crewe on the last operational Clyde turbine steamer, the *Queen Mary*, cruising from Gourock to Inverary, on the 44th anniversary of her first public sailing. *G. R. Hounsell*

Bottom: During the summer of 1978, in connection with the doubling of the line between Dalwhinnie and Blair Atholl on the Inverness-Perth main line, a regular service left Perth every weekday morning at 07.00 for Dalwhinnie. The train ran as 2N31 and was nicknamed the 'Welliboot' because it conveyed British Rail gangers engaged on the trackwork. It is seen here, to the south of Pitlochry, behind 25.239 on 31 July 1978. The train was made up of two conventional Mk I BSK and SK coaches, but also included the dining car from one of the East Coast main line Pullman sets, which had been disbanded several years earlier.

Engineering trains

Although most heavy engineering work is carried out at weekends, it is necessary to pre-place materials etc during the preceding week, ready for the occupation. The railway has a large number of permanent way depots spread all over the network, and it is from these that ballast hopper, track section and long welded rail trains are despatched from time to time to various destinations. Class 25s have always been regularly used on such duties because of their robust nature and because (being of route availability number five) they can go almost anywhere, as the following series of pictures will show.

Above left: A rare combination anywhere, but particularly so in East Anglia, 25.126 and 31.260, working in multiple, wait for a path at the exit of Chesterton Junction permanent way depot on 10 August 1982. They were in charge of the 8A26 09.53 SX Cambridge yard to Whitemoor up siding freight, which on this occasion conveyed only various engineers' spoil wagons.

Left: No 25.283 leaves Bescot yard on 27 April 1984 with a mixed rake of varying sized hoppers for reloading with ballast. The service is 7J02, the 10.15 SX to Blodwell quarry. *P. Kynaston*

Top: The guard pops his head out of the cab of 25.069 on 19 July 1983 as it approaches Chester from the Manchester direction with a two-wagon DCE trip. *P. A. Biggs*

Above right: With a train of long welded rail which had originated the day before from Hookagate depot near Shrewsbury, 25.270 passes the time of day in the loop opposite Hinckley signalbox, on 16 September 1982. It had to be regulated in this manner to enable the 12.25 DMU from Birmingham to Leicester to pass unhindered, as the passage of a long welded rail train is restricted to 25mph. *P. A. Biggs*

Right: Again at Hinckley, but this time travelling in the opposite direction, this is 25.089 on a Croft quarry-Nuneaton yard train of loaded four-wheel ballast hoppers, on 18 October 1983. *P. A. Biggs*

Left: No 25.146, fitted with miniature snow plough brackets, takes the inside of the curve on the relief lines at Barrow-on-Soar with a train of loaded fitted Mermaids, travelling from Croft quarry to Leyton permanent way depot in East London, 24 March 1982.
P. Kynaston

Below: No 25.263 prepared to leave Crewe TMD on Saturday 24 May 1980 with a 2Z99 17.55 crane special to Machynlleth. The following day it assisted with bridge repairs on the Cambrian line at Barmouth.

Left: In brilliant sunshine on 6 June 1982, the last Beyer Peacock-built Class 25, No 25.309, rests at Wrexham Crispin Lane siding, with a small engineers' freight from Mostyn docks, Deeside. *P. A. Biggs*

Below: The action takes place below Chester No 6 signalbox, as 25.253 eases a stone train from Penmaenmawr quarry to St Helens CCE depot, into Chester station. The busy yard pilot, 08.665, shunts a mixed trip, including Penyffordd-bound Presflos, alongside the box. In the background a further two Class 25s are visible stabled in the depot yard. *P. A. Biggs*

Above: No 25.035 speeds through Heaton Chapel station with an overhead electrification maintenance train on 19 June 1983. It was returning to Longsight depot after a long day's work near Cheadle Hulme, where the power supply had only recently been restored. *N. Johnston*

Below: A book without the obigatory Settle and Carlisle line shot would just not be on! Here, 25.297 is seen at Blea Moor whilst working a Ribblehead ballast on 7 September 1983. *Ron Cover*

A rake of four loaded airbraked Sealion ballast hoppers, emerge from New Mills tunnel on 9 July 1978, behind 25.327. This locomotive, the last in the series, is now, sadly withdrawn. *N. Johnston*

The demise

Recent years have seen the spasmodic withdrawal of more than two-thirds of the class, usually in bursts at the time of the winter and summer changes in the timetable in May and October. The vacuum-braked members of the class have usually been withdrawn without consideration of their condition or reliability — in other words, when main depot examinations have been well and truly overdue. Once withdrawn the locomotives usually tend to congregate at certain central points, from where spares are removed for re-use in an attempt to keep the rest of the fleet going for as long as possible. At Crewe, large numbers of the class, in condemned status, are robbed to enable other members on examination or under repair to be returned to traffic. Later, they are moved in groups of up to four at a time to Swindon where they are cut up. Although most of the class has now ended up at Swindon, certain members have been cut up elsewhere, for example at Glasgow works (if estimates for repair have been deemed too costly) or on site if involved in bad collisions. Withdrawn locomotives not on works premises at Derby, Glasgow or Swindon are still dotted all over the network, and at present some 20 specimens await their ends at Bath Road, Saltley, Crewe, Toton, Carlisle, Newton Heath, Polmadie, Healey Mills, Cricklewood, Tyseley and Springs Branch.

Below left: On 2 September 1982, 25.151 suffered brake failure whilst working a freight through Huddersfield. In an effort to stop the train it was diverted into a siding where it hit the buffer stops at quite a speed, as the damage clearly shows. The photograph was taken over six months later at Toton on 13 March 1983.
G. Grafton

Above right: A line of condemned Class 25/0s, 25.001, 25.013, 25.021 and 25.019, stand outside Swindon works near the dump on 2 November 1980. The four locomotives had arrived several days earlier from Millerhill, via York, with 25.001, although condemned, hauling them.

Right: The gutted shell of 25.052 stands coupled to a mineral wagon in Swindon works yard on 2 November 1980. To add insult to injury, the locomotive appears to have made the final part of its journey from the works 'A' shop to the dump with a set of redundant Class 08 buffers!

Below right: Withdrawn Western Region Class 25/2 No 25.225, stands beside the driving trailer of Southern Region EMU No 7184, outside 'A' shop in Swindon works.

Bottom: A study of 25.308 (the penultimate Class 25 built by Beyer Peacock at Gorton works) on the dump at Swindon works, where it resided for many months. It was standing between 25.187 and 25.097 when this photograph was taken on 23 April 1984.

Above: Nos 08.368, 25.120 and 46.016 stand in line behind Swindon works awaiting their ultimate fate on 23 April 1984.

Below: Two of the arrivals at Swindon, Nos 25.250 and 25.242, are seen here on Sunday 8 July, stabled in Cocklebury yard, awaiting transfer to the works after its annual summer holiday.